Volume 4

BRITISH RAILWAYS IN COLOUR

Alan Earnshaw & Kevin Derrick

Eastern

Nostalgia Road Publications

The **Famous Fleets** Series ™

is produced under licence by

Nostalgia Road Publications Ltd.

Unit 6, Chancel Place

Shap Road Industrial Estate, Kendal LA9 6NZ

Tel. 01539 738832 - Fax: 01539 730075

designed and published by
Trans-Pennine Publishing Ltd.
PO Box 10,
Appleby-in-Westmorland,
Cumbria, CA16 6FA
Tel. 017683 51053 Fax. 017683 53558
e-mail: admin@transpenninepublishing.co.uk

and printed by
Kent Valley Colour Printers Ltd.
Kendal, Cumbria
01539 741344

© Trans-Pennine Publishing Ltd. 2004
Photographs: As credited

Front Cover: Getting away from Newark, A3 Pacific 60046 *Diamond Jubilee* was another of the unsung members of this legendary class. Often overshadowed by its famous sister *Flying Scotsman* it is seen in June 1960. *Trans-Pennine Archive* (E320)

Rear Cover Top: A1 Class Pacific 60156 *Great Central*, is pushed in true Great Central style on the GNR main line to the north in May 1960. *Trans-Pennine Archive* (E251)

Rear Cover Bottom: Work-weary at Doncaster (36A) is J6 0-6-0, 64232, awaiting her next trip on 7th May 1960. *Frank Hornby* (E226)

Title Page: One of King's Cross Top Shed's stud of A4s, 60021 *Wild Swan* is found on a southbound special near Hitchin on 1st May 1963. This A4 was one of the group that was named after birds, and was not one of the nine 'Streaks' not to carry a plaque, motif or coat of arms. *John Newman* (E223)

This Page: Epitomising the Eastern Region A2/3 Class 4-6-2, 60523 *Sun Castle*, gets us away past the large King's Cross signal box. The 'new order' is already in the background, for by 21st May 1962 there is less than a year left for regular steam at the terminal. *Peter Coton* (E261)

ISBN 1 903016 32 0
British Cataloguing in Publication Data
A catalogue record for this book is available from the British Library

WELCOME to the fourth book in our new **British Railways in Colour** series, in which we consider the Eastern Region of British Railways. Like the previous three books in this series, we can only hope to give a flavour of the region under consideration, due to its vast size and complexity. It must be remembered that, when it was formed in 1948, the region covered the eastern half of England, stretching from the River Thames to the River Tweed.

Two parts of the Eastern Region always maintained an air of the pre-Grouped railways about them, and the Great Eastern and North Eastern sections always viewed that they should have been made regions in their own right back in 1948. Indeed, the NER's case was proved in 1956, when it was finally divorced from Eastern Region management.

Above: *The Gresley K3/2 Class had a large and distinctive six-foot diameter boiler, thereby giving a powerful 5P6F rating to the Mogul (2-6-0) wheel arrangement. In 1960 the class leader 61800 was allocated to Doncaster (36A), at this time and was a regular performer on the East Coast Main Line (ECML) at Gamston Bank.*
Trans Pennine Archive (E274)

In Volume Six we will tell the NER story in greater depth, and we will later return to specific sections of the Eastern Region and cover them more geographically and historically. However, for the present we now explore some of the sights and sounds of the region and the remains of its predecessor, the London & North Eastern Railway.

Above: After *Flying Scotsman* and the *Rocket*, A4 Class 60022 *Mallard* must be the third most famous locomotive name ever. She was one of many A4s to receive embellishments in the form of plaques or plates on their streamlined casing.; but hers naturally commemorated that famous dash down Stoke Bank on 3rd July 1938, when *Mallard* broke the World Steam Locomotive Speed Record.

There were several reasons for the record attempt, not least of which was to publicise the new express services that the LNER had progressively introduced from 1935 onwards when the A4 Class was launched. Streamlined trains and locomotives caught the public eye, but ironically it was the LMS who had taken the world record in 1937 when the locomotive 6220 *Coronation* had attained 114mph on the West Coast Main Line. Under the cloak of 'brake tests', Gresley decided to address both issues, as well as satisfy his sporting nature, 'to give the rivals a speed challenge which they would have little chance of beating.' His seven-vehicle test train was made up of three of the 'Coronation' twin sets, and the old North Eastern Railway dynamometer car, which made a total trainweight of 240-tons.

Starting just north of Grantham, they ran through the station at a modest 24mph, with the regulator wide open and a cut-off at 40%. The train then went up a 1:200 gradient for $2^1/4$ miles as it accelerated to $59^3/4$mph and for the next $1^1/2$ miles the cut-off was eased to 30% as the speed increased to 69mph. The final $1^1/2$ miles saw them climbing to the signal box at Stoke Summit, at $74^1/2$ mph. Fine work by Fireman Bray meant that Driver Duddington had all the steam needed for an unchanged 40% cut-off as the engine swept down the incline. From milepost 100, speeds at the end of each successive mile were increasing all the time until 125 mph was reached at milepost $90^1/4$.

During this section the dynamometer car's recording instruments revealed *Mallard* had also done a short distance at the tremendous speed of 126 mph, at which the 6 ft. 8 in. driving wheels would have been doing more than 500 revolutions a minute. Five mile posts (94 to 89) were reeled off at an average of 120.4mph and their speed actually exceeded 120mph for three miles continuously (posts $92^3/4$ to $89^3/4$). This view at Gamston Bank dates from the late Spring of 1961. *Trans Pennine Archive* (E293)

Top Right: As a result of the outbreak of war in 1939, the round 'World Record' plaque seen on *Mallard*'s casing was not fitted until British Railways days (in March of 1948). Once again smartly turned out by King's Cross (34A), affectionately remembered as Top Shed, *Mallard* is again at the same spot on Gamston Bank in the late Summer of 1962. The sharp-eyed will notice the differences (aside from up and down trains) in these two shots as two gangers are diligently at work keeping the grass under control on a bank where sparks would be expected in the days of steam. The second picture shows that there has been some regaining of the embankment by Mother Nature following some engineering work on this section. It will also be noticed that Mallard's nameplates are red in the previous picture and black in this.
Trans Pennine Archive (E202)

Bottom Right: Although the A4s were the most stylish locomotives on the ECML, they were not the only Gresley Pacifics, as this view of A3 Class 4-6-2, 60067 *Ladas* at Peterborough shows. These were perhaps one of the LNER's most famous designs, even though it had been modified by the time of this 1960 picture. This thoroughbred was named after the Lord Roseberry's Derby Winner in 1894 at odds of 2/9. Lord Roseberry was a former Liberal Prime Minister and Chairman of the British Linen Bank and intimately connected with various railways that became part of the LNER.
Trans Pennine Archive (E188)

Left: Staying with a Gresley theme (this time at Hitchin), we see V2 Class 2-6-2 60847 *St. Peter's School York A.D. 627.* Appropriately a York-allocated (50A) engine, she was one of only eight of the 184-strong class to carry a name; the naming ceremony being held at the ancient city's station on 3rd April 1939. Once again this view was taken on 1st May 1963 as the first withdrawals of this class were starting to be implemented. Also of note is the sighting panel, which has been applied on the brickwork of the bridge to aid with the spotting of a signal that has since been removed.
John Newman (E191)

Above: Our next V2, 60929, also displays a York (50A) shed plate as it stands on the inspection pits at Woodford Halse (1G) alongside Fairburn-designed 2-6-4T 42250. Although this depot had become part of the Midland Region by the time of our visit, the former Great Central Railway shed had been part of the Eastern Region up until the boundary changes of 1st January 1958. Formerly coded as 38E Woodford Halse is pictured here on 1st January 1964; some 16 months before the shed closed completely on 14th May 1965.
Win Wall, Strathwood Library Collection (E216)

Above: Here we pay a slightly earlier visit to Woodford Halse, and note that in this December 1962 picture the shed was coded as 2G and would retain this until 9th May 1963. This visit on what is obviously a freezing cold day, reveals the last working Gresley J39 0-6-0 64747 in what was her remaining few days at her home shed. In their heyday these engines could be found scattered right across not only the Eastern Region, but also on the former LNER lines of the North Eastern and Scottish Regions as well and often noted on passenger turns until the coming of the diesel railcars.

Of course, Woodford Halse will always be associated with the Great Central line, on which passenger services began on 15th March 1899. The GC quickly gained an excellent reputation and its train crews always viewed the world from an aloof position. The rival Midland route was circuitous and the LNWR wandered through the West Midlands. In contrast. the GC crews viewed themselves a unique breed, pushing their locomotives at great speed along their 'direct' straight main line.

Win Wall, Strathwood Library Collection (E192)

Top Right: Another last of class takes us to former Great Eastern Railway territory and Cambridge MPD (31A). We arrive there early one morning in 1959, to enjoy the sight of Holden's 1891-designed 2-4-0 62785 being prepared to work a special. Not only the last of her class, this little 71-ton locomotive is the last of her wheel arrangement at work on BR. Fortunately she was reserved for the National Collection and thus found sanctuary in the Museum of Transport at Clapham. The last surviving 4-4-2 Atlantic, 32424 *Beachy Head,* was not so fortunate a year earlier, as it was unceremoniously scrapped on the Southern Region in 1958.
Alan Pike OBE (E241)

Bottom Right: The Eastern Region had a sizeable number of pre-Grouping types, some of which could be found concentrated together in relatively small areas. As a result, the feel of a Victorian railway was never very far away. For example, T.W. Worsdell's 1883-design of the Class J15 0-6-0s were to enjoy a long life, even though more than half their number had gone after the coming of electric services to Colchester in the 1950s. Shortly before 65448 was transferred to her final shed Stratford (30A) in December of 1959, we see the locomotive alongside the soot-encrusted offices at Colchester (30E). It is doubtful that it ever went to 30A, for by March 1960 the engine was stored near Southend's Victoria Station before finding a place with the cutters at Stratford Works a month later.
Trans Pennine Archive (E208)

Above: Also seen at Colchester in 1959 is a B1 Class, 61363, which racked up five sheds in its last five years of service; the final shed was to be March (31B), where it was ultimately dumped for nine months from September 1962. It eventually moved away from the region to the Central Wagon Company's scrapyard at Ince near Wigan, but it was then to spend another seven months awaiting the last rites in January 1964. The electrification through this part of Essex witnessed an additional cost for providing wide gantries to span all the sidings, as it was intended to remove steam completely; even though electricity was only planned for passenger services in East Anglia at this time. The small cramped steam shed at Colchester was demolished in 1961 and a smart new diesel depot was provided instead. It supplied not only locomotives for the Clacton and Walton-on-Naze lines, but also shunters for Parkeston Quay and Harwich docks together with a host of small yards in Essex and Suffolk that required a resident shunter each day. *Trans Pennine Archive* (E265)

Right: The coming of the modern Britannia Class of Pacifics in 1951 saw the first batch of 15 engines being allocated to the Eastern Region, and this obviously preceded the arrival of the electrification at Colchester in 1959. However, it would not be long before the English Electric 1Co-Co1 Type 4 diesels (later known as Class 40) would take over the expresses in East Anglia and make the 'Brits' redundant in that area. Before their arrival, the now preserved 70013 *Oliver Cromwell* is found at Colchester with a mixed rake of Thompson and British Railways stock in October 1959. This former Roman garrison town was the junction where the Liverpool Street to Norwich (Great Eastern) main line met the branches from St. Botolphs, Brightlingsea, Clacton and Walton-on-Naze. All of these lines, except Brightlingsea that closed in 1964, remain open today in this not often photographed part of the Eastern Region. Note how these two views clearly show that the catennary is only supplied above the two main running lines! *Trans Pennine Archive* (B308)

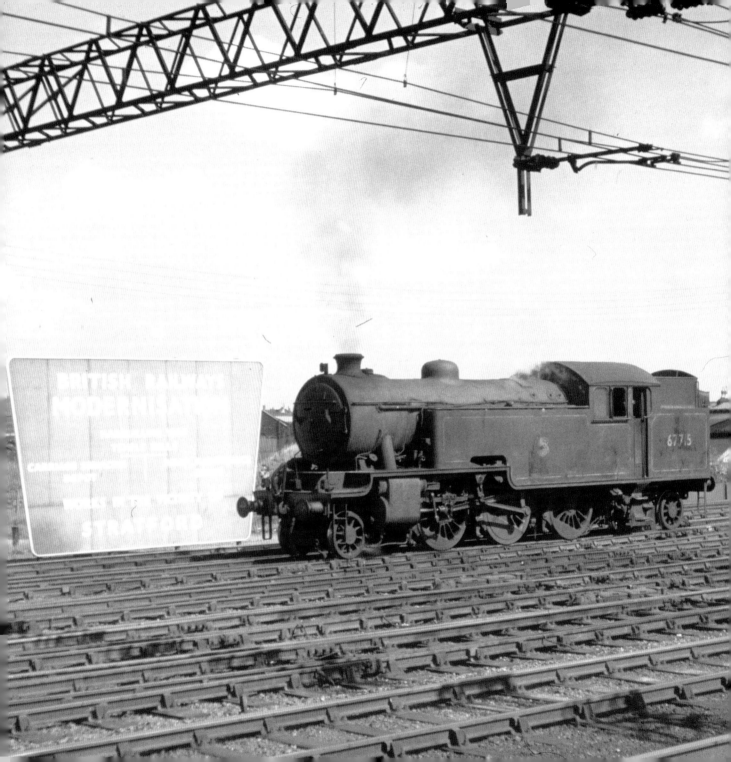

Left: The sign advertising modernisation around the Stratford area has clearly seen some sun, judging by the fading of the paintwork in this view from the station platforms. The locomotive in the picture, 67715, was from Edward Thompson's 1948-build of L1 Class 2-6-4 tanks at the LNER's Darlington Works, although the prototype went into traffic back in May 1945. Whilst it is seen performing one of the all too frequent light engine working's at this busy location, the class were often employed on outer suburban services from Liverpool Street before the electrification took real effect on their duties.
The Late Norman Browne, Strathwood Library Collection (E306)

Above: This L1 2-6-4T, 67737, has obviously been stopped a while at Stratford (30A) judging by the rust building up on her tyres. This was not an uncommon sight, and few of those who witnessed it will ever forget the large number of 'stored' locomotives that were building up at this location by the end of the 1950s! By the time of this shot in October 1961 Stratford Works was not only well into the swing of cutting up engines from the former GER and LNER, but had also started on those locomotives built after the nationalisation of the railways in 1948 – the oldest of which was a mere 13 years old at the time.
The Late Norman Browne, Strathwood Library Collection (E330)

Above: Modernisation at the end of the 1960s, and the rapid withdrawal of steam meant many changes. For example, the arrival of the diesel railcars on the Lea Valley routes and the electrification of the Liverpool Street suburban services sounded the death knell for the N7 Class 0-6-2Ts designed by A. J. Hill; these engines were built in several batches from 1914 with the last one being started in 1927. One of these, 69714 is seen 'stored' at Stratford in October 1961, having been officially withdrawn the previous month.

When Hill came to office in 1912 and introduced his first design the J68 later that year, he was obviously influenced by Holden's earlier Class J69/1 0-6-0 locomotives of 1902. By 1959, 59 such engines remained on the BR stock book, including 68563 seen at the top of the next page. The arrival of modern traction is also well illustrated by the DMU, which is resplendent with its 'cat's whiskers' lining on the front!

The Late Norman Browne, Strathwood Library Collection (E317)

Top Right: The J68s were very similar to Holden's creation, and further looked so when many of the J67s and J69s were rebuilt with Ross-pattern 'Pop' safety valves to replace the original Ramsbottom variety. In their early days these were the mainstay of the East London suburban passenger services and many were to survive 60 or more years although much of their service lives would be as shunters or trip goods engines in the many freight yards in the area at that time. This example, seen on 17th January 1960, would stay at work until that October before being rapidly scrapped a month later.
Frank Hornby (E340)

Bottom Right: Another area not very often covered in colour is the line to Shoeburyness at the head of the Thames Estuary; wouldn't it be incredible to find a colour image of the armoured trains that were based there during World War II? To compensate we do have a series of views at West Horndon, the first of these being of Stanier-designed 2-6-4T, 42530, which is one of the 37 three-cylinder locomotives introduced by the LMS from June 1934 onwards. Their arrival in Essex was part of an attempt to reduce the complaints from passengers on the former LT&SR routes over poor time-keeping. Praised for their rapid acceleration these engines were a success and were used on other lines as well. Here 42539 looks in a remarkably clean condition as it shows off the BR Mixed Traffic Locomotive livery!
David Knapman (M420)

Left: Taken on the same Whitsun bank holiday weekend of 20th May 1961 and based on a former Midland Railway design, this 4F Class 0-6-0 44228 was allocated to Cricklewood (14A) in North London. But it is shown here at West Horndon on Eastern Region metals as it brings another 'extra' packed with day-trippers for the seaside around Southend. The locomotives pictured on these pages are not of LNER origin, but neither were the LT&SR lines although these were transferred into the new management of BR after Nationalisation that brought the LMS routes logically (and geographically) under Eastern Region control. *David Knapman* (M457)

Above: The London Tilbury & Southend Railway originated in 1852 with an Act for a joint line, owned by the Eastern Counties (later GER) and London & Blackwall Railways. Trains initially ran in two portions, from Bishopsgate and Fenchurch Street stations, joining at Stratford. However, excursion traffic to Southend, soon became very important. Even as late as the 1960s, with very few people in the working class suburbs of London having their own cars, the idea of a day at Southend still seemed attractive. Despite being what is really a very muddy river estuary, another special heads to the resort behind 44297, an LMS 4F 0-6-0 from Cricklewood. *David Knapman* (M431)

Above: Congestion on the LT&SR through Stratford led to a diversionary route being built through Plaistow, which opened in 1858 and then became the main line with trains only running from Fenchurch Street. By 1862 the LT&SR had become a very profitable company and this led to its independence, although most of the directors were still appointed by the L&BR or the GER. When the lease expired in 1875 the company assumed the running of the line and acquired its own 4-4-2T locomotives and rolling stock, so that by 1880 the working of the trains by the GER had ceased. In 1882 the LT&SR became an entirely independent company, and in 1885-8 a new (shorter) main line was opened from Barking to Pitsea via Upminster. An extension to Shoeburyness in 1884 and the Romford to Grays line of 1892-3 completed the system.

Passenger traffic began to grow rapidly with the speculative London house builders opening new suburbs to the east of London, and secondly with people commuting into the city from the countryside or Southend as season-ticket holders. Tilbury docks (1886) boosted the small levels of goods traffic and also required boat trains for ocean liners. By 1912 the LT&SR was one of the nation's most profitable railways, but to the surprise of those who had forecast a takeover by the GER, it was bought by the Midland. Here one of the Stanier three-cylinder engines 42510 from Shoeburyness (33C) smokes heavily into the 1:132 climb away from West Horndon. The loading gauge seen on the right of the picture is a reminder that most stations expected rail borne goods traffic to leave their yards. *David Knapman* (M415)

Top Right: The initial objective of the LT&SR was, rather oddly, the heavy excursion traffic to Gravesend in Kent, and for this the railway leased the Tilbury-Gravesend ferry. By this they were able to compete with the South Eastern & Chatham Railway, and also avoid East Londoners having to travel via the city centre. Our visit to this link across the Thames is on 21st May 1960, as 4MT 2-6-4T 80096 allocated to Tilbury (33B) backs on to her train of rather sooty-looking coaches at Tilbury Riverside. This engine was the first in a batch of ten built from November 1954 at Brighton Works specifically for these routes. The scroll work on the station seat is an absolute delight and a far cry from those provided for travellers in the 21st century. For those interested in Thames pleasure craft, read the book *Steamers of the Medway and Thames*. *Strathwood Library Collection* (B223)

Bottom Right: Another British Railways Standard design from the drawing offices of Brighton was this 9F 2-10-0, 92140. It was the first of a small batch of ten locomotives that were built at Crewe in 1957 for the Eastern Region and provided with the higher water capacity of 5,625-gallon BR1F pattern tenders. Seen passing the wonderfully decorative fascia boards of Peterborough's North Box, it was allocated to New England (34E) as was this entire batch, save the one sent to Immingham (40B)! They would be a familiar sight to travellers overtaking them at speed on the ECML in the late-1950s and early-1960s. *Trans Pennine Archive* (B305)

Below: Derby Works was responsible for the design of the first BR Standard engines to arrive on Eastern Region metals in 1951. Ten years later some of them would still be at work from Liverpool Street, where we find Britannia Class 4-6-2 7P6F 70005 *John Milton* on the servicing and turntable roads of the smoky London terminus. The self cleaning SC plate is seen affixed under the Norwich (32A) shed plate, these would be dispensed with as time went on as engines went to sheds where perhaps supplies of the SC plates were not readily available.

All is in order on 14th April 1961, but how many enthusiasts of that day would reflect on the great Briton who inspired the engine's name? John Milton (1608-1674) was one of the greatest poets of the English language, and is perhaps best known for his epic work *Paradise Lost* (1667). Milton's powerful rhetorical prose and the eloquence of his work had an immense influence especially on the 18th-century verse. However, in addition to his poetry, Milton also published pamphlets defending civil and religious rights. *Strathwood Library Collection* (B228)

Above: This ex-works Thompson B1 Class 4-6-0, 61252 also has its SC plate firmly affixed ready for a resumption of work at Stratford on 7th May 1959. She would return to traffic at Ipswich (32B) but would move again five times before ending her days as a running locomotive at March MPD (31B); but this was not quite the end of her service.

It was at that depot that 61252 would become Departmental Locomotive No.22 from November 1963 and used for steam-heating purposes. The end would finally come at King's scrapyard in Norwich in July of 1966, by which time 61252 was in a disgraceful state.

Simon Coombe, Strathwood Library Collection (E318)

Above: Right up until the mass-scraping in the private yards in the mid-1960s, most engines would normally stay in their usual working area , until they went for scrap at the works that had looked after them through their working lives. This would certainly be the case for many locomotives based around Sheffield where we see another B1 4-6-0 61360 on a special working under the wires at Sheffield Victoria in 1966.

Migrating away from the East Anglian lines in late-1959, after the electrification, she settled at Doncaster (36A) and was often seen at work in the Barnsley area until her withdrawal came in April 1966. It lingered around the shed for a further three months before a trip off Eastern Region metals to Cohen's scrap yard at Cransley near Kettering in August 1966.

Trans Pennine Archive (E307)

Below: Edward Thompson, best appreciated for his B1 Class, also had his hand in the design of A2/3 Pacific 60514 *Chamossaire*. These locomotives went into traffic just as he was retiring and A. H. Peppercorn was developing the design to become the A2 Class, which had a slightly shorter wheelbase. The rim-less chimney still fitted to *Chamossaire* is very distinctive if not attractive.

This New England (34E) machine is pictured here as it is simmering in the shed yard at Hitchin (34D). Fortunately this was an easy shed to photograph, as it was right alongside both the station and the mainline. She would wait her turn as stand-by in case of diesel failures on 4th May 1962, in what was the last full summer of steam at the southern end of the ECML. *Peter Coton* (E189)

Left: Taken on that same Summer day at Hitchin we find Sir Nigel Gresley's A3 Pacific 60047 *Donovan* on the through lines with an express. She, or should it be he, has been modified with the German style of smoke deflectors but retains the original Great Northern type of tender. This is perhaps another mismatch of styles, as when fitted with the later LNER tender and deflectors these engines looked 20-years younger! *Donovan* incidentally was not named after the British version of Bob Dylan who was to become popular with musical successes in the 1960s. Rather, like many of her class, *Donovan* was named after a famous racehorse of the day, which in turn it is said had been named after the famous British naturalist Edward Donovan. *Peter Coton* (E314)

Above: We next see Hitchin on 19th May 1961. The locomotive 70041 *Sir John Moore* was from the second batch of Britannia Pacifics delivered to the Eastern Region by Crewe Works, where it was out-shopped in March 1953. The locomotive is interesting as two John Moore's, father and son, may claim the credit as being Great Briton's. The father was born at Stirling in 1729, and his novel *Zeluco* produced a great impression on and influenced the poetry of Byron, and thus left an abiding mark on English literature. His eldest son was General Sir John Moore who is well-known in British military history as a result of the Peninsular War, the Egyptian Campaign and the Napoleonic Wars.
Frank Hornby (B309)

Top Left: We now travel south down the ECML to Welwyn North. Looking back towards the station, aside from joining a few spotters on the platform to see the passing of A1 Pacific 60126 *Sir Vincent Raven*, our eyes drift to the five garages on the right of the picture. These were provided at the back of the goods yard for the benefit of passengers who wished to leave their cars in secure, covered accommodation. Welwyn was of course a famous new town of the 1930s, with that attractive name of 'Garden City' being devised by the marketing people in order to draw people out of London to live in the outer suburbs. Today's commuters travel from stations further north than Welwyn, and indeed come from much greater distances along the Great Northern Railway's main line. Classic examples would be Peterborough and Newark, but the fast GNER trains also bring people to the city on a daily basis from much further north.
John Newman (E312)

Bottom Left: Climbing up the embankment at Welwyn for a better view of the passing trains we can also see the goods yard and warehouse in the distance. The signal post is a wonder to behold, an eclectic mix of lattice and timber post, carrying arms for both up and down trains. The 9F is another of the Eastern Region's allocation of engines from 1954, and 92037 was still allocated to New England (34E) in 1963. This engine would find further work out of Immingham (40B) after New England closed to steam in April 1965.
John Newman B328)

Above: This Swindon-built 9F 2-10-0, 92183, shows considerable evidence of lime-scale deposits from the safety valves and around the front end, presumably due to the hard water supplies at its home shed New England (34E). This depot had no less than 40 members of the class allocated there at one time or another and had originally been a main shed coded 35A until 1958. Many visitors to the shed would have opted to take the bus rather than face the 40-minute walk from Peterborough North Station. Six of the shed's 9Fs were to be withdrawn from New England as were six A4 Pacifics too, although this would happen a few years after 10th April 1960 when this visit was made.

Frank Hornby (B179)

Above: If there was one type of locomotive that was associated with New England more than 9Fs, it would have to be the Austerity 2-8-0s; with 59 being allocated at various times in the 1950s and '60s. This engine, 90246, moved further north to Retford (36E) in October 1963 when the Brush Type 2 diesels absorbed their work around Peterborough. In the background on the same day can be seen Type 2 diesels from the North British Locomotive Company, which had been in store here for two months.

Later known as Class 21s, these pilot scheme diesels were plagued with engine troubles and therefore largely unwanted by the Eastern Region. Later these locomotives, re-engined by Davey Paxman of Colchester, moved to Eastfield (65A) on the Scottish Region. Even so the class only remained operational until the end of 1971 when they were sold for scrap. The 2-8-0 managed a longer overall service life, even though it went to Arnott Young at Dinsdale in July 1965 for dismantling. *Frank Hornby* (B201)

Below: The large number of 9F engines to be found at New England would often draw photographers to get a shot of these heavy freight machines in glorious colour. The proportions of the BR1F tender with 5,625 gallons of water capacity are to be seen here to full advantage. One can only imagine what the proposed 6,000-gallon tender for a batch to be allocated to the Southern Region may have looked like, but this proposal was never implemented.

Interestingly, this locomotive is reputed to have received a boiler that had originally been intended for BR's last steam locomotive, 92220 *Evening Star*, which became spare and was fitted to 92180 at Darlington during an overhaul. Seen on shed on 9th May 1964 this 9F moved away from New England the following month. Regretfully, none of these machines ever fulfilled the working lives that R A Riddles CBE had expected. *Strathwood Library Collection* (B242)

Below: One named engine that would end its days on the books of New England was A3 Class Pacific 60106 *Flying Fox, which* is seen in May 1964. Kept very clean at this point, her service career would however only last another seven months working north from here. During this time it would occasionally be seen on pick up goods trains of all things, but what a way to use 6ft 8in driving wheels! The first batch of Sir Nigel Gresley's glamorous Pacifics were designed and ordered by the Great Northern Railway prior to the formation of the LNER. Before the Grouping Gresley had already built two Pacific engines and these were the true forerunners of the A3 Class, and also the flagships of the company. As 1474, *Flying Fox* was the first of her class to be named after a racehorse in April 1925. It is a pity that, even though the LNER had fitted fox embellishments to A4 *Silver Fox* and the D49 Hunt Class, they did not work out something decorative for this engine too?

Win Wall, Strathwood Library Collection (E331)

Above: The Manchester, Sheffield & Lincolnshire Railway, formerly the Sheffield, Ashton-under-Lyne & Manchester, undertook the construction of the first Trans-Pennine railway. Taking a main line through the Pennines, and creating the world's longest railway tunnel at the time, the MS&LR created a route that defied some very arduous terrain. The company later extended its line east towards the Humber and west, through the Cheshire Lines Committee to the Mersey. It also proposed a brand new line southwards through the East Midlands and the Home Counties, making it the last main line to reach London.

It was this scheme that led to its change of name as the Great Central Railway. The GCR built their locomotives at the Gorton Works and one of these was the N5 Class 0-6-2T locomotives that were introduced by T. Parker in 1891. Nearly seven decades later, on 10th April 1960, 69293 finds a last bit of work as a shed pilot at New England. These engines had a flowerpot chimney and tall dome cover, which gave the class a dated but definite GCR family look. In earlier days of BR, the 121 members of the N5 Class would have been a common sight all over the region.
The Late Norman Browne, Strathwood Library Collection (E324)

Above: Whereas the N5 retained its old GCR features, a more familiar Gresley look was imparted to both V2 2-6-2 60902 (with inside steam chest) and N2/4 0-6-2T 69587. The V2 was of course a World War II creation, built at a time when there was an embargo on building express locomotives. To circumvent this, Gresley turned to the design for a 2-6-2 Mixed Traffic engine that he had introduced in 1936, and built these in substantial numbers. The N2 however, was of a much earlier design and dated from 1928, although in turn this can be traced back to Gresley's days with the GNR.

This particular sub-division of the class was fitted with condensing apparatus and a smaller chimney as they were intended for working the Moorgate lines in London, which had been built to a more restrictive loading gauge than that found on the Metropolitan Railway. Large sand boxes were also fitted to help prevent too much slipping in damp or wet tunnels. Many of these N2s were to be seen at New England, but they were also allocated to duties from many of the steam sheds that came under King's Cross (34A), though a sizeable allocation was based in Scotland too.
Frank Hornby (E352)

Below: Spalding Town hosts an O2/4 Class 2-8-0, as 63948 has stopped for a much-needed refill to its tender from one of the platform-mounted water cranes. As can be seen, the Gresley look is again obvious, thanks to the Great Northern pattern of smoke box door. Viewed after a light rain shower, this station once lay at the hub of lines in the Fens, with those from the Peterborough to Boston (GNR) and March to Sleaford (GNR/GER Joint) serving the town. In addition these lines were connected by spurs to the Midland & Great Northern Joint Railway's cross-country line that passed ain an east-west direction just south of Spalding. This was a once busy spot for goods workings, albeit very seasonal in its nature. For example it would receive much extra passenger and express-rated freight traffic each year during the annual flower and bulb growing seasons, whilst the Autumn saw trains packed with fresh vegetables, potatoes, and seeds.

Strathwood Library Collection (E319)

Left: With the coming of the GNR in 1848, coastal shipping from Boston declined and the port's prosperity evaporated. Well into BR days Boston boasted its own engine shed (latterly coded 40F). However by the time of this view on 24th April 1965, the shed had been closed for 16 months. This was followed during the 1960s by the closure of much of the railway network in Lincolnshire, as the Beeching 'axe' bit deeply into the rural areas. This Thompson B1, 61406 is seen heading a Nottinghamshire and Lincolnshire LCGB special over many of the lines scheduled to be closed. Engines were changed at Boston on the tour, and the large number of these passengers are for the special and sadly not for the service trains.
Strathwood Library Collection (E364)

Above: Another of the widespread B1s, 61390, is seen on a return to New England MPD on 21st May 1963. Based in this area all of its working life at either Immingham or Colwick, this 4-6-0's service career was to be ended by a trip to Birds of Long Marston in July 1966. Regretfully, only one of the class made it to Woodhams Yard at Barry and as a consequence the balance between preserved Black Fives and B1s is not particularly healthy if you favour Eastern Region engines. This sad fact of life is in spite of there being a far greater number of named B1s than there was in the Black Fives. There were a number of interesting contrasts between the LNER's 'maid of all work' and its LMS counterpart, sadly it is difficult to demonstrate these in preservation. *Michael Beeton* (E193)

Above: Taking the route back towards March (31B) on 10th April 1960, we find Class O2/3 2-8-0 63975 laid up in the yard where it is slowly gathering rust on its tyres. March shed with its adjacent Whitemoor marshalling yards was to take over the importance in the area from the Peterborough shed of New England, with the yard here becoming one of the most important marshalling points for freight movement in the whole country, before its eventual rundown. During the war years, 1939-1945, Whitemoor had seen a phenomenal level of traffic associated with the many aerodromes in East Anglia, but it was an earlier World War that had led to its creation. Whitemoor was part of German war reparations and consisted mainly of a huge marshalling yard that was modelled on the Ham yards of Germany; today a prison has been built on the site!

It was from Whitemoor that a train loaded with bombs left for White Colne (on the Colne Valley & Halstead Rly.) on Friday 2nd June 1944. The 390-yard long train, drawn by WD 8F 7337 stopped twice en-route for the crew to examine its deadly load; but, as it passed through the town of Soham the fireman, Ben Gimbert, noticed that the leading wagon was on fire. Despite the risks to their own safety, prompt action by Gimbert, his driver James Nightall and the Soham signalman, James Bridges, a cataclysmic explosion was averted when they divided the train. Soham was thankfully saved from a major disaster, but the leading wagon exploded killing both Nightall and Bridges. Ironically, whilst Gimbert and his guard, Herbert Clarke, survived the disaster of 1944 they both died in 1976.

The Late Norman Browne, Strathwood Library Collection (E363)

Top Right: The arrival of the WD 2-8-0s in East Anglia saw a change in motive power that continued after the war, and as seen previously the ex-WD engines became prolific in the 20 or so years following VE Day. Even so, the older GCR, GER, GNR and LNER types were not completely ousted, but telling the various types of LNER 2-8-0s apart without the aid of an ABC was not an easy task for those who were brought up in areas where these engines were not an integral part of the daily scene. The ABC tells us that 63890 is an O4/7 with a shortened O2 type boiler, but retains the Great Central smokebox. This version does appear to be gainfully employed on that same visit to March shed in April 1960.
The Late Norman Browne,
Strathwood Library Collection (E194)

Bottom Right: The LNER 2-8-0s continued to be used on what were traditionally heavy trains. This included those that hauled coal and steel around the Lincolnshire town of Frodingham, which was firmly in Great Central territory and on the line promoted by the MS&LR from Sheffield to the south side of the Humber. On 12th June 1932, the new Frodingham locomotive yard was opened in Scunthorpe by the LNER. It is at Frodingham MPD (36C) that we find 63884, which with care can be identified as an O4/8; it is fitted with a B1 type boiler, but retains the original GCR cylinders. Most of these 2-8-0 varieties found work on the local iron ore trains, before being usurped by both English Electric Type 3 and Brush Type 2 diesels. *Len Smith* (E247)

Above: During World War I, the GCR 2-8-0s were favoured by the Government as being the ideal locomotives for the Railway Operating Division. This class of locomotive, designed by Robinson, had been introduced in 1911 with a small boiler, Belpaire firebox, with steam-operated brakes and water scoop. Those taken into war service performed so well that a modified version, without water scoop, was built for the ROD. Many of these saw service overseas, and on their repatriation they were purchased by both the GCR and the GWR. Under the LNER the design was perpetuated through different variations, with the last being rebuilt from 1944 onwards with a larger 100A boiler; the type that was used on the B1 Class. These became known as the O4/8 Class, one of which is 63878 seen at Worksop working an east-bound train loaded with coke on 2nd January 1964. The O4 rebuilding programme was of course an economic solution for the LNER, before the arrival of the scores of War Department 2-8-0s that were to follow.
Win Wall, Strathwood Library Collection (E266)

Right: Despite the concentration of heavy industry, and its prolific coal traffic in many areas, the LNER covered a very large part of the country with lines that could never have been truly profitable. The services on these lines were kept buoyant by the highly profitable routes, but in times of economic difficulties it was hard to sustain this cross-service support. To alleviate its shortage of locomotives, the hard-pressed LNER purchased several of these 0-4-0T chain-driven engines from the Sentinel Wagon Works at Shrewsbury from 1925. Many of those in Classes Y1 and Y3 later went on to become Departmental Locomotives and renumbered in a style favoured by the Eastern Region for many of its locos. These oddballs were interesting to many spotters of the day who sought them out, as for example No. 42! Here it is captured in the care of The Civil Engineering Department, along with an old match boarded Pullman coach, secreted away at Chesterton Junction near Cambridge in March 1960.
Alan Pike OBE (E203)

Below: Doncaster Works was the final resting place for several life-expired 'Departmental Locomotives'. Here a J50 Class 0-6-0T, formerly 68928, is seen carrying the hapless Departmental No.13. It might have prolonged its life for a short while, but it has finally run out of luck when pictured at Doncaster in 1965. Cold and lonely, it awaits scrapping at the works with another J50. Once upon a time, these venerable 0-6-0Ts were scattered right across the former LNER lines of the North Eastern and Scottish Regions too. Designed by Sir Nigel Gresley for the Great Northern Railway they dated from 1922.

In August 2003, Doncaster Works, currently owned by Wabtec plc, celebrated its 150th anniversary. As the reader can well imagine, in a century and a half building and refurbishing engines and rolling stock, the works have gone through a few incarnations. The Plant, as it is known locally, has been the birthplace of 2,500 locomotives and thousands of carriages and wagons. Some of the most famous, like the *Flying Scotsman* and the *Mallard* returned to celebrate the recent anniversary. However, some of once numerous classes built there were sadly conspicuous by their absence. *Len Smith* (E195)

Above: Another engine that was broken up at Doncaster Works, this time in October 1959, was 61633 *Kimbolton Castle*. These LNER-built 4-6-0s were named after various stately homes, regiments or football clubs, and thus gave the locomotives much interest. Here the B17/6 is seen against the decorative canopies at March station, it is one of the class with B1-style boilers. Again, note the comparison with modern canopies (if you can find them on stations today), as the difference between elegance and economy is obviously noted.

Kimbolton Castle, near Huntingdon, was originally a medieval castle, but underwent many changes before the Great Rebuilding by Vanbrugh, Hawksmoor and Adam. It was the country house of the Dukes of Manchester, but the Castle's most famous resident was Katherine of Aragon (one of the wives of Henry VIII), who died there in 1536. Small sections of the Tudor house that she would have known have survived down to today, although the castle is now a public school.

Trans Pennine Archive (E224)

Below: The concept of naming locomotives was really a publicity policy by the railways, and by association with commonly known places, people, animals, army regiments or buildings, the LNER achieved this goal. Whilst *Kimbolton Castle* would be easily recognised by people in Cambridgeshire or students of Tudor history, it may well have been lost on a wider audience. The same was not true with the B17 Class engines that carried the names of football teams, these being taken from the top teams of the day. Today teams like Darlington, Doncaster Rovers, Hull City and Huddersfield Town may be in the lowly Third Division, but back in the 1920s they were in the top flight.

Huddersfield, for example had won both the FA Cup and the Division One Championship (three times) in the 1920s, and they regularly shared honours with Arsenal. Meanwhile, Arsenal's London neighbours, West Ham United, although recently relegated from the Premier League, also had the distinction of seeing 61672 named after the club. In the 1950s this engine was shedded variously at Stratford (30A) as seen here on 7th May 1959, and also at Ipswich (32B) and Lowestoft (32C). She was relegated to scrap at Stratford Works in March 1960, not too far from the 'Hammers' ground at Upton Park.

The Late Norman Browne, Strathwood Library Collection (E234)

Above: Another great name from footballing history was Bradford City, which had a tremendous following by generations of people who worked in the local woollen textile industry. Great rivals with other top West Riding of Yorkshire clubs, like Huddersfield Town and Leeds United, the premier Bradford club (the other was Bradford Park Avenue) had its name fixed to a B17/4 Class engine. These were introduced in 1936 with a 4,200-gallon tender, whereas the B17/6 were re-builds of the B17/5 introduced in 1937 with the streamlined casing, but later fitted with the 100A boiler like the B1 Class. Sadly these footballers did not work regularly in the areas where the teams, who they denoted, played their home matches. For instance, 61668 *Bradford City* was shedded at Stratford (30A) with a short spell at Colchester (30E) in 1959 before becoming redundant. At this time many of the new electric multiple units were still to go into service, so steam lasted a while longer than was planned. Originally the lines out of Liverpool Street to Shenfield were electrified by the LNER at 1500 volts DC, but they were converted to the British Railways standard of 25,000 volts AC to match the remainder of the new scheme. *Trans Pennine Archive* (E196)

43

Above: Famed for the brass football incorporated into their nameplates, the 'footballers' were a big draw for youngsters of the day! Alan Earnshaw recalls that it was a must to 'cop' all of these in his train-spotting days, and as a matter of fact his *ABC Combined Volume* for 1959 has just one omission, 61660 *Hull City*. Yet one of the biggest teams of the era, Newcastle United, saw its name being carried for just two weeks in 1936 by 2858. The engine was promptly renamed as *The Essex Regiment* and thereafter carried their crest. Switching between Stratford (30A) and Colchester (30E), the last battle for the re-numbered engine (61658) was lost at the hands of Doncaster's cutters in February 1960. *Trans Pennine Archive* (E255)

Right: The former spit and polish of the pre-Grouping era was recaptured on J69/1 Class 0-6-0 68619, when it was repainted at Stratford into a smart version of the original Great Eastern Railway livery. The crews had the chance to polish up the burnished metal in between their turns of duty as one of the Liverpool Street pilots, and they thus copied the pre-Grouping livery station pilots that appeared on the North Eastern Region at that time. Liverpool Street Station had a real reputation for being a 'real dark hole', although the electrification scheme helped relieve the smoke. However, with an office tower built above it today, the station sees even less daylight than it did on 13th May 1960. *Frank Hornby* (E248)

Left: In what is a truly atmospheric picture, we see B1 Class 4-6-0 61042 getting away from Liverpool Street with her train in June 1960. At this time the B1 was allocated to Lincoln (40A), but she had no less than seven sheds in her last ten years of service! Consequently, one suspects that her steaming capabilities were not good, as one foreman after another sent her packing in the hope of receiving a better replacement. Even Doncaster Works sent her packing off to Cohens of Kettering in July 1966, after 'The Plant' stopped its scrapping program.
Alan Pike OBE (E342)

Above: Local goods work was often the preserve of 0-6-0s such as Holden's Great Eastern Railway Class J19 from 1912. One of these, 64656, was a long term resident of Stratford but it is seen here at Colchester, shuffling about with her drain cocks open in 1959. Stratford Works ensured that very little evidence remained of 64656 within days of its official withdrawal in May 1960, as the cutters were ruthlessly efficient to the last. The buildings in the background, save for the World War II 'pill-box', do not seem to have an air of permanence about them either.
Trans Pennine Archive (E190)

Above: As previously mentioned, the Eastern Region had a love of stationary boilers, so they made much use of locomotives that were no longer considered 'roadworthy'. Where the defects did not extend to the boiler, it was decided that a locomotive could be used as a stationary engine. These were often tucked away around the back of engine sheds or in carriage sidings, where they were used for steam-heating purposes; in this case we see an example at March MPD (31B). It is one of Holden's 1901 rebuilds of the J16 Class 0-6-0s; ironically with the fitting of round top fireboxes to create the Class J17.

This example, 65541, was to officially act in this capacity from July 1962 until January 1964 and (as can be seen in the picture) it was therefore connected up to a regular supply of water and given an outlet for its steam. The crude chimney extension is of a height to create a better draught and cause less smoke nuisance, and not done to impress the spirits of George Stephenson or Timothy Hackworth. The picture also shows that her running days are well and truly over, as she was already in harness as a stationary boiler in this view taken on 15th January 1962.

Strathwood Library Collection (E249)

Above: A Great Eastern Railway type dating from even earlier than 65541 was also giving good value as one of the last few of Worsdell J15 Class engines. These 0-6-0s had been designed by the GER in 1883, and in turn been modified by J. Holden; three of them (65391, 65405 and 65424) had even been given a side-window cab for working on the Colne Valley & Halstead Railway. By 7th May 1959, no less than 47 J15s still survived, but only a few of these would be hanging on as late as 1962 . The example shown here, 65464, was to be one of the final four of this class broken up in March 1963.

This particular engine was a long-term resident at Stratford (30A), but in the earlier days of British Railways they were allocated across ten sheds in East Anglia, with some of the engines working to furthest reaches of their areas thanks to their maximum route availability and light axle loading. As the GER's Yl4 'small goods' class 0-6-0, they were designed to haul coal trains on the newly opened GN-GE Joint line from Doncaster. When the 289th Y14 appeared from Stratford Works, it made this numerically the largest class on the GER; of that total, 19 were built by Sharp, Stewart. *The Late Norman Browne, Strathwood Library Collection* (E204)

Below: A chronic locomotive shortage existed on the LNER at the end of World War II, as many engines were either beyond their 'life-expectancy' or prematurely ready for withdrawal as a consequence of their high mileage and inadequate maintenance between 1939 and 1945. Still some distance from Nationalisation, the LNER began a building programme centred on types that had been introduced in the 1930s. These build programmes continued after 1st January 1948, and one such was Thompson's K1 Class of 1945, which was a rebuild of the K4s that Gresley had introduced for Scottish traffic in 1937.

In 1949 A H Peppercorn sanctioned a new build of K1s with an increased length and slightly lower engine weight. One of these 2-6-0s, 62013, is seen here on her home shed of Stratford in the many rows of engines always to be found at 30A on days like 7th May 1959. A year later things would be changing rapidly, but more modern engines such as this K1 would still find a few more seasons work out of sheds like Frodingham (36C) near Scunthorpe. October 1963 saw her dropping her fire for the last time, although Frodingham retained a steam allocation until 27th January 1966.
The Late Norman Browne, Strathwood Library Collection (E267)

Above: The removal of steam from the Great Eastern section was undertaken with remarkable haste, and old favourites such as the GER Claud Hamilton Class D16s were scrapped with an almost indecent rush. One of these old-timers, who worked its last turns from March (31B), was 4-4-0 62517. Previously she had been a Yarmouth Beach (32G) engine, but with all three Yarmouth sheds closing in 1959 (the others were Vauxhall and South Town), the writing for the D16 was on the wall. As this was in the period before Stratford Works stopped cutting up engines at the end of 1961, the D16s were consigned to their birthplace.

At Stratford Works, these crack express locomotives of their day were to be swiftly disposed by the cutting lines. In fact the scrap team had already claimed 66 of the 68 D16s that had been withdrawn prior to 1957, and had usually done the deed within a month of an engine's official withdrawal. The remaining two made it to Manchester, but there was no reprieve there, as the Gorton Works dealt with them similarly. This view of 62517 is just days away from the end at Stratford and it has the look of the Death Row about it, despite the tender full of coal.

The Late Norman Browne, Strathwood Library Collection (E235)

Above: It was the lure of the main line and not the scrap yard that would capture most enthusiasts' attention back in the 1960s. Indeed, engines like A2/3 Pacific 60520 *Owen Tudor* also provide the opportunity to spend a sunny afternoon photographing trains at a favourite vantage point such as here just south of Hitchin. With the absence of much of today's background noise, and with just the sounds of the birds and the breeze to be heard, the distinctive sound of an approaching train could be gauged from some distance if the conditions were right. Furthermore, in the days before orange vests and Personal Track Safety Certification, sitting on a railway embankment such as this was regarded less of a trespass or threat than it would be today. The working is a special in connection with an Ocean Liner on 1st May 1963. Also of further interest are the sleepers spaced across the cess. *John Newman* (E332)

Above: To those lineside observers, the sound of a chime whistle in the distance would herald the periodic arrival of one of Gresley's immortal A4s to enliven the scene for a brief moment. On the sunny day in 1963, it is the turn of 60032 *Gannet* to sweep a King's Cross to Newcastle express under the footbridge towards the spectator's position. At this late stage in the A4's stay at the Top Shed, and just before transfer to New England (34E) for her last four months in traffic, *Gannet's* condition is more typical of Gateshead shed (52A) rather than the earlier years it spent in London. By the end of 1962 all the A4s were ousted from King's Cross, and 60003 *Andrew K. McCosh*, 60014 *Silver Link*, 60028 Walter K. Whigham, 60030 Golden Fleece and 60033 *Seagull* were all sent north to meet an unceremonious end at Doncaster.

John Newman (E297)

Above: The early 1960s were a major time of change, and the sight of K3s on the main lines passed to history. Indeed, when this shot of 61958 was taken in 1959, the 2-6-0 had been relegated to marshalling empty stock at Ipswich. With the end of steam in sight for Lowestoft MPD (32C), this engine transferred to join others at the former Great Central shed in Staveley (41H). However, this was followed very smartly by a move to Mexborough (41F) in the South Yorkshire coalfield and her withdrawal from service a few months later. By 1962 the monthly lists (in *Trains Illustrated* or *The Railway Observer*), which showed the numbers of steam engines being withdrawn, were reaching plague proportions. All too quickly diesel railcars spread throughout East Anglia, only to be followed by many of the branches closing soon after their arrival. The various Type 1 diesels from both North British and British Thomson Houston, along with many diesel shunters' working trips, also coincided with the progressive withdrawal of goods facilities. Along with the north of Scotland, Norfolk and Suffolk were the first counties to become both steam-free and rapidly railway free thereafter.

Trans Pennine Archive (E205)

Above: Before long, the distinguished lines of the B12 Class 4-6-0s would almost go the same way as the D16s, with Stratford Works calling them all back for an indecently fast conversion to scrap metal; save the preserved example 61572. This class member, 61535, was allocated to Ipswich (32B) and then transferred (on the books at least) in its last month of service November 1959 to Norwich (32A). However it seems highly probable that she did not make it to Suffolk, and as her time was already up, Stratford received this B12 in December, and quickly cut it up alongside 61571 the following month.

It is seen here in the last few months of duty, undertaking the more menial task of shunting a train of newspaper and postal vans at Ipswich in 1959. At the start of that year 22 had been in stock, but the class was rapidly reduced as the year progressed. It should be remembered that Sir Nigel Gresley rebuilt the class from a Holden GER design of 1911, with the first one coming out of the works in May 1932. Thereafter they were capable machines and well suited to the task of working heavily loaded trains such as The Continental, which ran between Liverpool Street and Harwich. *Trans Pennine Archive* (E242)

Above: The combined tender-cab layout of this, the very last E4 class 2-4-0, displays great practicality in an engine first conceived nearly 70 years earlier. The class had been designed by Holden on the GER back in 1891 and was 17 strong on Nationalisation in 1948, with an allocation spread between Bury St. Edmunds, Cambridge and Norwich. However, by the time that the Ian Allan *ABC Combined Volume of British Locomotives* was published in 1959, there was just one survivor, 62758, which is seen here in close-up at Cambridge station on 16th May 1959. The final three E4s had in fact all been concentrated on Cambridge (31A), and these Victorian relics were often to be seen working on the branch to Mildenhall or on local stopping trains to Colchester. January 1960 was her last month on British Railways, however there were several specials arranged by various societies including OURS (Oxford University Railway Society) to see out the class in style.
Frank Hornby (E333)

Top Right: The coal piled into the bunker of N7 Class 0-6-2T, 69715, looks like it may well need plenty of breaking up in this view taken on 7th May 1959. The picture also shows that rough shunting may have been the cause of the dent in the cab-side. With all of the hundreds of engines stabled at sheds like Stratford (30A) over the weekends, sometimes locomotives would be left fouling point work and not seen until it was too late. This was especially so when a yard shunter pushed a long line of engines after dark in order to free others from the rows. So busy were these locations, that to get to record everything 'on shed' on a Sunday could take several hours in 1959 such as when this visit found the yard packed to capacity.
The Late Norman Browne, Strathwood Library Collection (E197)

Bottom Right: Formerly named *Newcastle United*, B17/6 4-6-0 61658 *The Essex Regiment* has the compact style of tender that held 4,200 gallons of water when full. Unlike 69715 this B17/6 appears to be loaded with a tender full of 'ovoids' whose sub-standard burning characteristics would not be welcomed by a driver and fireman having a rough run. Although it is in lined green livery, layers of acquired soot and grime cover this once prestigeous engine and it fails to bring any credit to the proud regiment whose name it bears. Note that 61658 still carries the earlier 'cat on a mangle' totem on the tender, whereas the engine next to it has the newer style.
Trans Pennine Archive (E334)

Top Left: The modifications to A3 Pacific 60047 *Donovan* that we mentioned earlier in this book are only partially complete in this view that was taken at King's Cross Station Loco Yard. It will be seen that the A3 has, however, gained its 'banjo-style' dome and double chimney, even though the standards of cleanliness have again started to slip. Also of interest is the brightly glazed mess bothy that had been provided for the yard. It contrasts well with the superb Victorian gas-holders that dominated the overall scene at this location.
Frank Hornby (E225)

Bottom Left: Talking of the unkempt state of BR engines at the end of the 1950s, or early-1960s, we can illustrate this with a picture of a Britannia Class Pacific in 1961! Although just ten years old, 70002 *Geoffrey Chaucer* was already unwanted by the Eastern Region. Demoted from the top link at Stratford, it was sent to Yarmouth Town in January 1959 and then sent to Norwich in February 1959. It did almost two years on the Norwich diagrams, but it spent the winter of 1960/1 as a spare engine and was sent as surplus to March in June 1961. It is pictured just after its arrival at March in 1961, but its use was in question and by July 1963 it was stored at the shed for the rest of the year before being finally handed over to the London Midland Region and Carlisle Kingmoor (12A) at the start of 1964. Although the Eastern Region was keen to 'modernise' its locomotive fleet, there can be no excuse for the way in which engines were turned out by the mid-1960s. *Trans-Pennine Archive* (B202)

Top Right: As one of the last survivors of the BR Brittania Class, 70013 *Oliver Cromwell* was a real celebrity in the last weeks of steam on British Railways. She will of course also be rembered as one of the stars of the 30-Guinea Special, in BR's August 1968 tribute to steam. In those days it was polished and buffed up to look like the front line express engine that it still was, but the state in which it had been operated by Eastern Region when it was still a relatively new engine was a disgrace; as proved by this picture at Stratford (30A) on 7th May 1959. Contrast it with the newly outshopped tender in BR's mixed traffic livery alongside.
The late Norman Browne,
Strathwood Library Collection (B304)

Bottom Right: Thus far we have concentrated mainly on the southern end of the Eastern Region, primarily because we have future volumes planned to cover both West and South Yorkshire, Nottingham and so on. However, to show you one of the northern outposts of the Eastern Region, we travel north to Rotherham's Masbro Station near the boundary between the Eastern and North Eastern regions. This was very much Midland Railway territory for many years, even in to BR days, but in this 1961 view we can see the new order has arrived with a short inter-regional express from Leeds to Derby. Here a BR Standard 5MT, 73031, pauses to pick up passengers, as an ex-MR 3F 0-6-0 (out of picture) takes a mixed rake of loaded and empty wagons through the station.
Trans-Pennine Archive (B341)

Above: *Coming back to where we started, A3 Pacific 60105 Victor Wild, complete with double chimney and German-style smoke deflectors coasts past the King's Cross signalbox and into the platforms under the watchful gaze of young enthusiasts.* Strathwood Library Collection (E210)

EVERY PICTURE is worth a thousand words, or so they say, and thanks to the combined talents of photographers who have supplied material to both the Strathwood and Trans-Pennine archives, we have a lot to say in future volumes. Of course it would not have been possible to tell this story without the kind co-operation of the contributors named in the credits shown in this book. To those and all those who captured British Railways In Colour, we say a massive thank you! However mere words are never enough, and we hope that the ongoing series will provide a testimony to their far-sighted work.

In conclusion, can we offer a reminder that all of these published shots are available to purchase as superb duplicate slide copies direct from Strathwood. The code number at the end of each slide indicates its catalogue number, and also the name of the photographer whose work we felt warranted inclusion.

To get your copy of the extensive catalogue listing of these and many thousands of other shots available in fabulous colour, please send £5.00 to: -

> Strathwood Limited
> Kirkland House, Bruce Street, Whithorn.
> Dumfries & Galloway DG8 8PY

Or visit the websites: -

www.strathwood.com or www.railwayslide.co.uk.

In return we will send the collector's catalogue, complete with sample slide, post free to UK addresses (overseas add £2.50).